Country Dezeebob C

Skeeta's

AKA: Mosquito
Jokes and Cartoons
about <u>all</u> bugs and insects
Over 140 Pages and 300 Illustrations

Desi Northup
The Cartoon Guru

Made in the USA

Published in the United States by Desno Publishing Co. All rights reserved. No part of this book may be reproduced in any manner whatsoever without written permission from the publisher, except in the case of brief quotations from articles and reviews. Artwork is, also, not to be duplicated or reproduced.

Desno Publishing Co.
Route 3 Hopkinton NH 03229
Copyright 2014 Desi Northup

What's a potato bug's favorite class?

Mashematics.

Why did the stinkbug call the restaurant?

To place his odor.

Do sand flies like the beach?

They shore do.

What vehicle do bees drive?

A Hummer.

~ 4 ~

How many bees were in the bee choir?

A humdred.

What do you call a bee born in May?

A maybe.

Happy Birthday!

What do insects learn in school?

Mothematics.

What's green and dangerous?

A caterpillar with a bad temper.

Why was the little insect crying?

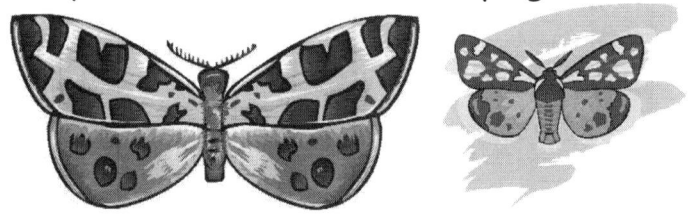

It wanted its moth-er.

What do you get when you eat caterpillars?

Butterflies in your stomach.

Where do fleas go to surf?

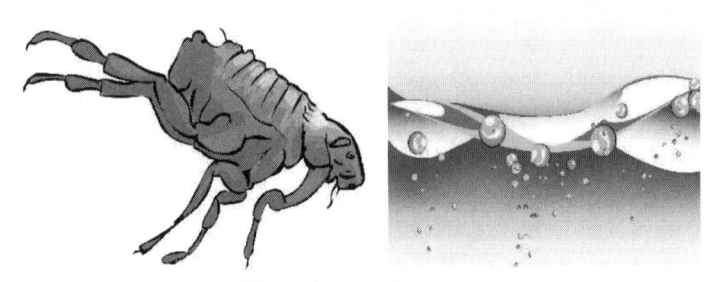

To the micro-wave.

How can you tell if a dog has artistic fleas?

If he has artistic fleas, he is always 'etching'.

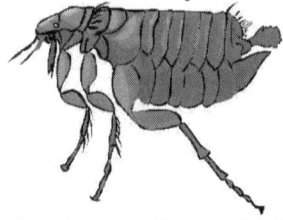

What did the bumble bee say to the Venus fly trap?

"Hello, honey."

Which bug crows at sunrise?

A clockroach.

How can you tell if a cockroach has been at the movies?

By the popcorn stuck in his teeth.

What's the easiest way to catch a cockroach?

Have someone through it at you.

When do flies celebrate with a big meal?

Garbage day.

Why do flies chase garbage trucks?

They love fast food.

What should you do if a fly lands on you pizza?

Give it a pizza your mind.

How do flies get their groceries home?

In lunch bags.

Why are flies good at chores?

They like to take out trash.

What should you do if a fly lands on your sandwich?

Read it a bedtime story.

What did the fly do when it fell into a bowl of chicken soup?

Used its noodle.

Why do flies take so many baths?

They have sticky feet.

What has leaves and flies?

A Venus fly trap.

Why are bees so sweet?

They are always in the sugar bowl.

Should you shoo flies?

No, let them go barefoot.

Why did the fly fall into the mustard?

It couldn't ketchup with ants.

What did the frog say to the fly that got away?

"Catch you later."

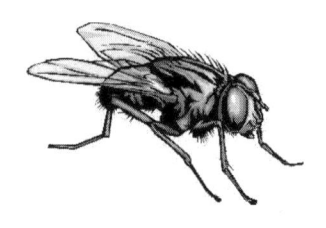

What do you get if you cross a fly with a hippo?

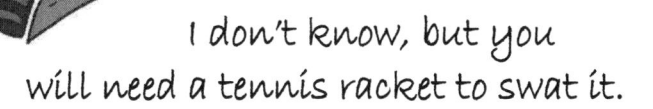

I don't know, but you will need a tennis racket to swat it.

What did the mosquito say the first time he saw a camel?

Did I do that?

When are mosquitoes most annoying?

When they get under your skin.

What carries a sucker and bounces up and down?

A mosquito with the hiccups.

How can you tell mosquitoes are tame?

They eat right out of your hand.

What do you get if you cross a mosquito with a hippo?

I'm not sure, but if it bites you, you'll be in big trouble.

Diner: "Waiter, there is a dead spider in my soup."

Waiter: "Yes, sir, they aren't very good swimmers."

What should you do if your pet mosquito is hungry?

Take it out for a bite.

What happens when a girl mosquito meets a boy mosquito?

It's love at first bite.

What has eight legs and goes up and down?

A spider in an elevator.

What do you get if you cross a bee with a skunk?

An animal that stinks and stings.

What do you get if you cross a centipede with a chicken?

Enough drumsticks to feed an army.

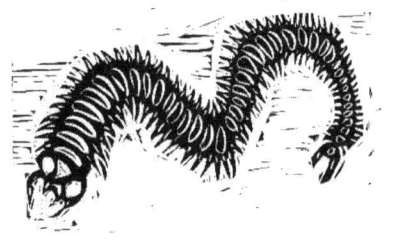

What do you call a mayfly with criminal tendencies?

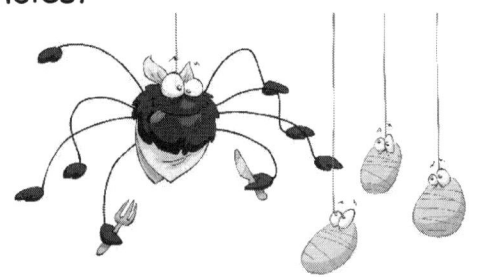

Baddy longlegs.

How do mosquitoes travel?

They itch-hike.

What's a mosquito's favorite sport?

Skin diving.

What do you call an Irish mayfly?

Paddy longlegs.

What are the most faithful insects?
Bees. Once they find friends,

they stick to them.

Who can leap tall poodles in a single bound?

Super Flea!

What do you do when two snails have a fight?

Leave them to slug it out.

What did one insect say to the other?

Stop bugging me.

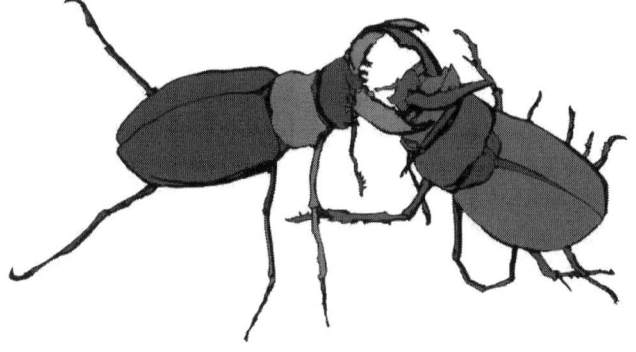

Why was the mother flea unhappy?

She thought her children were all going to the dogs.

What did the clean dog say to the insect?

"Long time no flea."

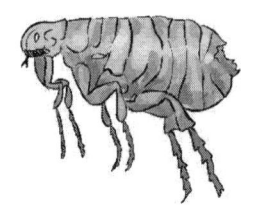

How can you find where a flea has bitten you?

Start from scratch.

How do bugs relax in the tub?

They take bug-gle baths.

How do butterflies wear their hair?

In ponytails.

Why was the insect thrown out of the forest?

Because he was a fire bug.

What happened to the two bugs that fell in love in the winter?

They got married in the spring.

How do you make a tick laugh?

Tickle it.

What kind of bugs live in a dogwood trees?

Bark beetles.

What did one slug say to the other who had hit him and run off?

"I'll get you next slime."

What was the snail doing on the highway?

A bout a mile a week.

What kind of bugs live on pussy willows?

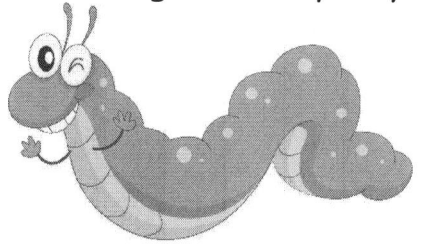

Caterpillows.

What's a caterpillar's favorite sandwich?

A peanut butterfly and jelly sandwich.

What is the definition of a slug?

A snail with a housing problem.

What is a definition of a snail?

A slug in a crash helmet.

What did the apple tree say to the hungry caterpillar?

"Leaf me alone."

What do caterpillars play while spinning their cocoons?

Wrap music.

Where does a traveling bug spend the night?

At a roach motel.

Which bug has a roof and a chimney?

The housefly.

What do you call a greedy ant?

An anteater.

Who was the most famous ant scientists?

Albert Antstein.

What's made of leather and has laces and wings?

A shoe fly.

Why was the camper so upset?

He had ants in his plants.

Why did the ants elope?

Nobody gnu.

What do you call an ant with frog's legs?

An ant-phibian.

What did the ant foreman shout to his crew?

Let's hop to it, guys.

What lives in a swamp and has lots of children?

Mas-quitos.

What do you call a chick ant?

Eleg-ant.

What do you call an ant that likes to be alone?

Independ-ant.

Why was the firefly flashing on and off?

His light was on the blink.

What goes clump, clump, clump ouch?

A centipede stubbing his feeeet.

If ants are so busy, how come they

THE ANTS EAT MORE OF YOUR PICNIC THAN YOU DO.

always have time to show up at picnics?

What's a best part of a bee?

Its knees.

What do you call money saved by a stinging insect?

A hornet's nest egg.

Which bug can tell your fortune?

The gypsy moth.

What is red and dangerous?

Strawberry and tarantula jelly.

Which line did Bugsy Shakespeare write?

"To bee or gnat to be."

Why did the princes Fly scream?

She saw a dragonfly approaching.

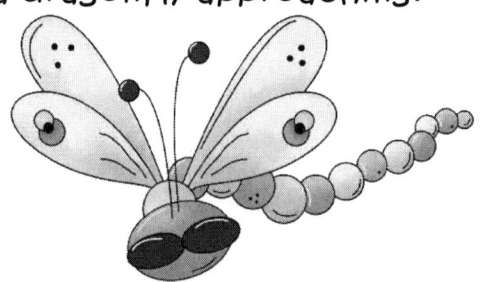

What did the slug say to the other slug who had hit him and run off?

"I'll get you next slime."

How do you know your kitchen floor is dirty?

The slugs leave a trail on the floor that reads "clean me".

What goes boing, boing, boing, splat?

A grasshopper crossing a busy street.

Which dance do spiders do in Hawaii?

The Tarant-hula.

What kind of mattress does the ruler of a beehive sleep on?

Queen size.

What do you find at the end of a bug's foot?

Mosqui-toes.

How did the bee find a job?
He looked in the want ads

of the fly paper.

Where did Jack and Jill Bug go to fetch a pail of water?

Up an anthill.

What do you find in a spider's baseball glove?

Lots of webbing.

What is the silliest bug?

The cuckoo-roach.

What do you call a lady spider who never gets married??

A spin-ster.

Which pass route did the football spider run?

A fly pattern.

Which bug do you find in churches?

The praying mantis.

How does a flea travel?

They 'itch-hike.

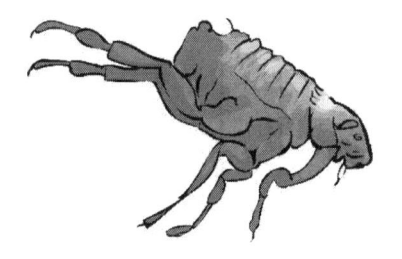

What do you call a rabbit with fleas?

Bugs Bunny.

What do you call a bee who's had a spell put on him?

He's bee-witched.

What did one centipede say to the other centipede?
"You've got a lovely pair of legs,
You've got a lovely pair of legs,
You've got a lovely pair of legs,
You've got a lovely pair of legs,
You've got a lovely pair of legs,
You've got a lovely pair of legs ..."

Why didn't the two ants go on Noah's Ark in an apple?

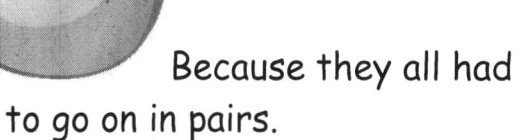

Because they all had to go on in pairs.

Why did the worm keep stealing things?

He was light fingered.

What is the best advice to give to a worm?

Sleep late.

Why did spider woman buy a car?

So she could take it out for a spin.

What is the most faithful insect?

A flea, once they find someone they like they stick with them.

What insect runs away from everything?

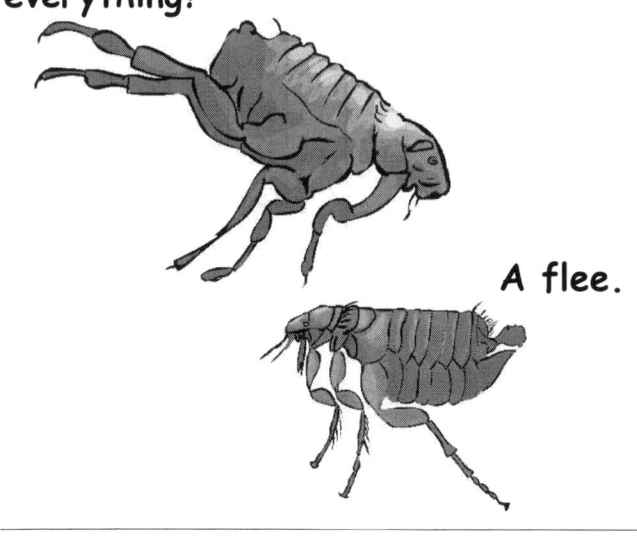

A flee.

What did termite do when she couldn't carry the twig on her own?

She hired an assit-ant.

What do you get if you cross a spider and an elephant?

I'm not sure, but if you see one walking across the ceiling, you'd better run before it collapses.

What do you get when you cross
A walrus with a bee?

A wallaby.

What did one firefly say to the other?

So long. Got to glow now.

What do you call a cheerful flea?

A hop-timist.

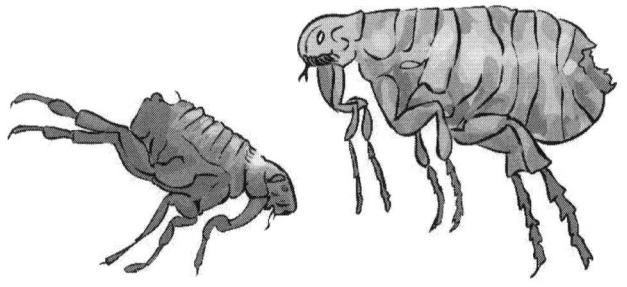

What did the dummy do to the flea in his ear?

Shot it.

What do you get if you cross a worm with an elephant?

Big holes in your garden.

Why did the ant travel to the South Pole?

He wanted to visit the ant-arktic.

If there are 5 ants in the kitchen how do you know which one is the football player?

The one in the sugar bowl.

What is the difference between a fly and a bird?

A bird can fly but a fly can't bird.

A golfing duffer cringed when his ball landed in an anthill. Choosing a sand wedge, he swung at the half-buried ball. Sand and ants flew. The ball hadn't moved. Again the novice swung. Again the anthill was devastated, but the ball lay unmoved.

Among the panic-stricken ant colony, one ant yelled, "Come on gang! That big white ball seems to be a pretty safe place to hang out."

What kind of bug does a cowboy ride?

A horsefly.

What kind of insects do campers like?

Fireflies.

A boy went to the drug store and bought a box of mothballs. The next day he returned and bought a second box. When he came back the third day, the clerk commented, "You sure must have lots of moths in your house."

"Yes I do," admitted the boy, "and I can't take it anymore. I've been throwing these balls at them for two days, and I haven't been able to hit a single one."

All they do is throw them back.

What is a baby bee?

A little humbug.

What do caterpillars do on New Year's Day?

Turn over a new leaf.

Where do ants go on a vacation?

Frants.

What do you call a 100-year old ant?

An antique.

A cricket walked into a London sporting goods store.

"Hey," said the clerk, shocked to see an insect with interest in sports. "We have a sport named after you."

"Really?" said the cricket.

"You have a game called Frank?"

What do you give a 300-pound mosquito?

Your left arm.

As Noah and his family were disembarking from the ark, they paused on a ridge to look back. "We should have done something, Noah," his wife said. "That old hulk of an ark will sit there and be an eyesore on the landscape for years and years to come."

"Everything's been taken care of," Noah assured her wife.

"I left two termites aboard."

What kind of bee is always dropping the football?

A fumblebee.

What do you call a bee what hums very quietly?

A mumblebee.

Some Boy Scouts from the city were on a camping trip. The mosquitoes were so fierce, the boys had to hide under their blankets to avoid being bitten. Then one of the boys saw some fireflies and said to his friends:

"We might as well give up. They're coming after us with flashlights."

What do you call a 100-pound mosquito?

Sir.

What did the mother grasshopper say to her children?

"Hop to it!"

What kind of insects can dance?

Jitter-bugs.

The hand is quicker than the eye is,

But somewhat slower than the fly is.

What did the fly say to the fly paper?

"I'm stuck on you."

What did King Arthur called his pet insects?

The Gnats of the round table.

What kind of bugs do knights fight?

Dragonflies.

What did the boy say to the mosquito?

"Don't bug me."

What has 18 legs and catches flies?

A baseball team.

What lives in a store and jumps over shelves?

A grass-shopper.

How many night crawlers are there in a foot?

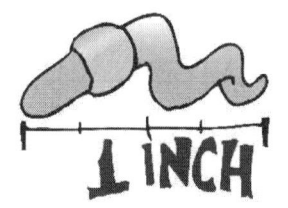

Twelve inchworms.

What kind of insects sleep the most?

A bedbug.

What kind of bugs are the best singers?

Hum-bugs.

Little Miss Puckett
Sat on a bucket
Eating some pancakes and cream.
Along came a grasshopper
And tried hard to stop her,

But she said,
"Go away, or I'll scream!"

What did the slug say as he slipped down the wall?

"How slime flies."

What is the name of a famous bug rock group?

The Beetles.

What kind of bugs are the messiest?

Litterbugs.

How do the French transport their snails overseas?

In es-cargot ships.

How do escargots cross the ocean from France?

By snail boat.

As one snail said to another,

"Your pace or mine?"

A waiter was bringing food to the table of her customer, a moth. She tripped and then said to the moth,

"Ooops sorry. I made the butter fly."

What's the difference between a run-down hotel and a banner for a hive? One is a flea bag,

and the other is a bee flag.

What likes to spend the summer in a fur coat and the winter in a woolen bathing suit?

A moth.

What lives in a hole, has horns, and runs really fast?

An ant-elope.

Behold:

what bee wrestlers use in matches.

Mammoth:

the mother of all butterflies.

Why didn't the butterfly go to the dance?

Because it was a moth ball.

Why didn't the bug feel like doing anything?

Because it was a slug.

Myth: a female moth.

There once was a fellow from France
Whose hobby was searching for ants,
Till he took quite a spill
In a tiny red hill
And wound up with ants in his pants.

What is a world's largest insect??

A mammoth.

What happened to the worm when it didn't clean its room?

It was grounded.

What is grey, buzzes, and eats cheese?

A mouse-quito.

The snail said to the turtle,

"What's the rush?"

There was a woman who loved the bees.
She always was their friend.
She liked to sit upon their hives,

But they stung her in the end.

How does an amoeba say good-buy?

With a microwave.

Why did the mosquito wake up in the middle of the night?

It was having a bite-mare.

What did the mother firefly say to her husband while looking at their son?

"He's bright for his age, isn't he?"

Knock, Knock!
Who's there?
Bee.

Bee who?
Just bee yourself.

Who wore a coonskin cap and played a British game?

Davy Cricket.

Why did the firefly cross the road?

Because the light was with her.

How do you start a flea race?

"One, two, flea, go!"

Knock. Knock.
Who's there?
Amos.
Amos who?

Ouch! Amos-quito bit me.

As the firefly said,

"When you gotta glow, you gotta glow."

A mother fly and her daughter were walking across the head of a bald man, when the mother observed, "How quickly times change. When I was your age, this was just a footpath."

Why did the flea live under a dog's chin?

He wanted a woof over his head.

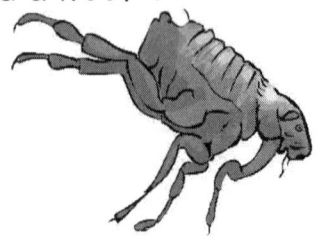

Knock, Knock!
Who's there?
Bug spray.
Bug spray who?

Bugs-pray they won't get squished.

Did you hear about the guy who went fly-fishing?

He caught a two-pound fly.

Why do some insects have a knack for swarming around you when you start a picnic?

Because flies time when you are having fun.

What did one night crawler say to the other night crawler?

"I know this great place down the road where you can eat dirt cheap!"

Why did Sir Lancelot need a can opener?

Because he had a bee in his knight clothes.

What is a bug's favorite band?

The Beatles.

What kind of paper is best for making kites?

Flypaper.

Did you hear about the mathematical flea?

They add to your misery, subtract from your pleasure, divide your attention, and multiply like crazy.

How did the flea travel around the country?

By Greyhound.

What kind of bugs read the dictionary?

Spelling bees.

One caterpillar said to another when
they watched a butterfly float by,

"You will
never get me up in one of those things."

Young termites are babes in the wood.

Old termites never die.
They just live happily ever rafter.

What is the menace of the bug world?

The weevil empire.

Where do you take a hornet when it's sick?

To the wasp-ital.

Why don't cockroaches make reservations at nice hotels?

They like the crumby places.

What is a bee's favorite bird?

A buzz-ard.

When he found bugs feasting on an embalmed body, the Egyptian undertaker said,

"Mummy is the loot of all weevil."

Did you hear about the worm that joined the marines?

He wanted to be in an apple corps.

Did you hear about the caterpillar's New Year's resolution?

It promised to turn over a new leaf.

Why are snails one of the strongest creatures in the world?

They carry their houses on their backs.

What is high-strung cocoon?

A wound-up caterpillar.

What did the worm say to her daughter when she came home late?

"Where on earth have you been?"

"Man, how slime flies!"

Macintosh apple: "What's the matter? What's eating you?"

Granny Smith apple: "Worms."

Bookworm – a person who would rather read that eat,

or a worm that rather eat than read.

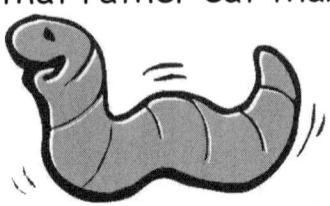

What do you call a fly with no wings?

A walk.

How high can a bumblebee count?

To a buzz-illion.

Mosquito -

an insect that bites the arm that feeds it.

Why did the amoeba cross the biology lab?

To get to the other slide.

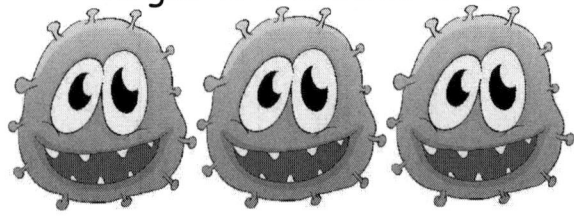

What did one bee say to the other bee on a hot summer day?

Sure is swarm, isn't it?

How do sick insects arrive at the hospital?

In an ambul-ants.

What goes "snap, crackle and pop"?

A firefly with a short circuit.

Why are mosquitos religious?

They prey on you.

How do you start a flea race?
By shouting, "One, two, flea, GO!"

What is the highest rank in the insect navy?

Flea-t admiral.

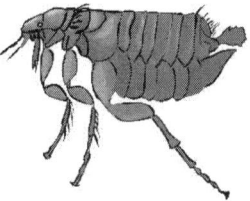

What is the biggest ant in the world?

Elephant.

What did the little centipede say to his mother when they went shopping?

I need a new pair of shoes. And a new pair of shoes. And a new pair of shoes...

How do you keep flies out of the kitchen?

Let your dog poop in the living room.

What size meals do glow worms prefer?

Light meals.

Why did the flea live on the dog's chin?

He wanted a woof over his head.

Why is honey so scarce in Boston?

Because there is only one B in Boston.

Some say the fleas are black,
But I know that just ain't not so,
"Cause Mary had a little lamb

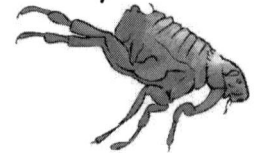

With fleas as white as snow.

What do bees wear when they go to work?

Buzzness suits.

Then there was the guy who's not a very good artist,

but he sure draws flies.

Why will the computer ever replace the newspaper?
You can't swat flies and line the bottom of a birdcage with a computer.

How do you find where a flea bit your dog?

Start from scratch.

How do bees get to school?

School buzz.

What has four wheels and flies?

A trash can.

What do you call a well-dressed ant?

Eleg-ant.

What is more amazing than a talking dog?

A spelling bee.

My pet store only sells ant farms and rabbits. What do you call your shop?

The Bugs Bunny Store.

What's the favorite song in a hive?
"Bee it ever so humble,

there's no place like comb."

What do nuts chase after with little nets?

Peanut butterflies.

What is a myth?

A female moth.

Do you ever take your ant farm out for a walk in the summer?

No. But sometimes
I take them to a picnic.

What is a bug's favorite kissing game?

Spin the beetle.

What is a bug's favorite questioning device?

A fly detector.

What do you call a guard with 100 legs?

A sentrypede.

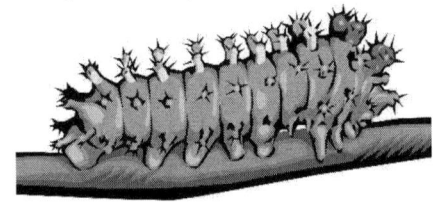

Why did the queen bee kick out all of the other bees?

Because they kept droning on and on.

When did the bee get married?

When he found his honey.

What do you have if you cross a pet spider with a pet hare?

A pet webbit.

What goes "zzub, zzub?

A bee flying backwards.

Did you hear the joke about the man who was accidentally bitten by the star flea in a flea circus?
The doctor ordered him to recuperate for a week. During his time off, he visited Hollywood and won a small part in a film. He thus was the first person to become an actor because he was bitten by an acting bug.

What is a bug's favorite fall drink?

Apple spider.

What does a bug do after it has a cold?

It disinsects its room.

What arachnid is like the top of a house?

An attick.

Where do sick hornets go?

To the waspital.

What did the bee say to a naughty bee?

Bee-hive yourself.

What do you call a mosquito in a metal suit?

A bite in shining armor.

What do you call two spiders that just got married?

Newlywebs.

What goes 99-clonk, 99-clonk, 99-clonk?

A centipede with a wooden leg.

What insect can leap over fourteen cans of bug spray?

Weevil Knievel.

When we think of caterpillars,

we get a worm fuzzy feeling.

How do bugs make up their minds?

They pestdecide.

What did one firefly say to the other?

"I got to glow now."

If a moth breaths oxygen in sunlight, what does it breath at night?

Nightrogen.

What is the last thing to go through a bug's mind when he hits your windshield?

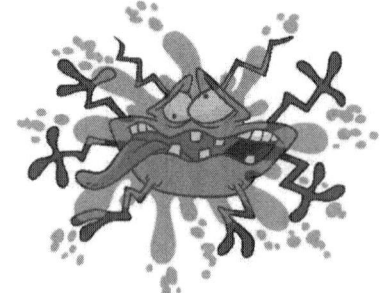

His butt.

What do you call an ant with five pairs of eyes?

Antteneye.

What is worse than finding a worm in your apple?

Finding half a worm.

Two worms met coming out of their holes in the ground.
"I think I'm in love with you," gushed the first.
"Don't be ridiculous," replied the second.

"I'm your other end."

Did you hear about two silk worms that were in the race?

Neither won because they ended up in a tie.

How does a caterpillar start its day?

It turns over a new leaf.

Boy: "That's your pet? That big, ugly, hairy, scary tarantula?"

Girl: "Yes. Isn't he adorable?"

Why is a letter A like a flower?

Because a B always comes after it.

Did you hear about the worker bees that went on strike?

They wanted more honey and shorter flowers.

What do you get when you cross a bee with a sheep?

A Baa Hum-Bug.

What kind of party does a flea go to?

A fleaesta.

How did the bee get off the web?

It turned off the computer.

How can you recognize police glow worms?

They have blue lights.

What do you call a 100 year old ant?

An ant-ique.

What do bees do with their honey?

They cell it.

Did you hear about the beekeeper who processed honey in the blender and whipped it into a foamy fountain of sticky sweetness?
He videotaped the process and send it to the TV show

"America's Honeyest Foam Videos."

What did one flea say to the other flea?

"Should we walk or take the dog?"

Why is bee's hair always sticky?

Because it has a honeycomb.

What do bees love to chew?

Bumble gum.

What's even more dangerous than being with a fool?

Fooling with a bee.

What do insects take when they are ill?

Anti-bee-otics.

Did you hear about the entomologist?

His job drove him buggy.

What did one worm say to the other worm?

"Where in earth have you been?"

What did one bee say to the other bee on a hot summer day?

"Swarm, isn't it?

Did you hear about the female bedbug?

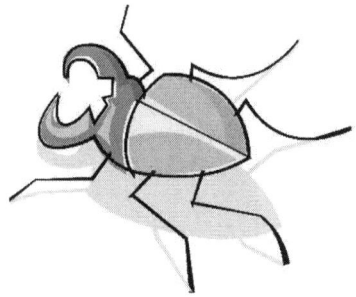

She had a baby in the spring.

A caterpillar is an upholstered worm.

Why do spiders spin webs?

They don't know how to knit.

What kind of bugs like toast?

Butterflies.

What did the bee say when it was working very hard?

"I'm buzzy."

How do bees travel?

By buzz.

This book *is another publication in the **Chromicals**™ series; a trademark of Desno Publishing Co.*

Chromicals ™

Description of an object, word, phrase or event presented and displayed in a manner with continually changing font sizes and styles, accompanied by an illustration that further defines the description of that subject, generally with a degree of comic relief.

You can Find these and Many other BOOKS by DESI NORTHUP either ON-LiNe or at a Bookstore Near you.

Desi Northup
The Cartoon Guru

Country Dezeebob